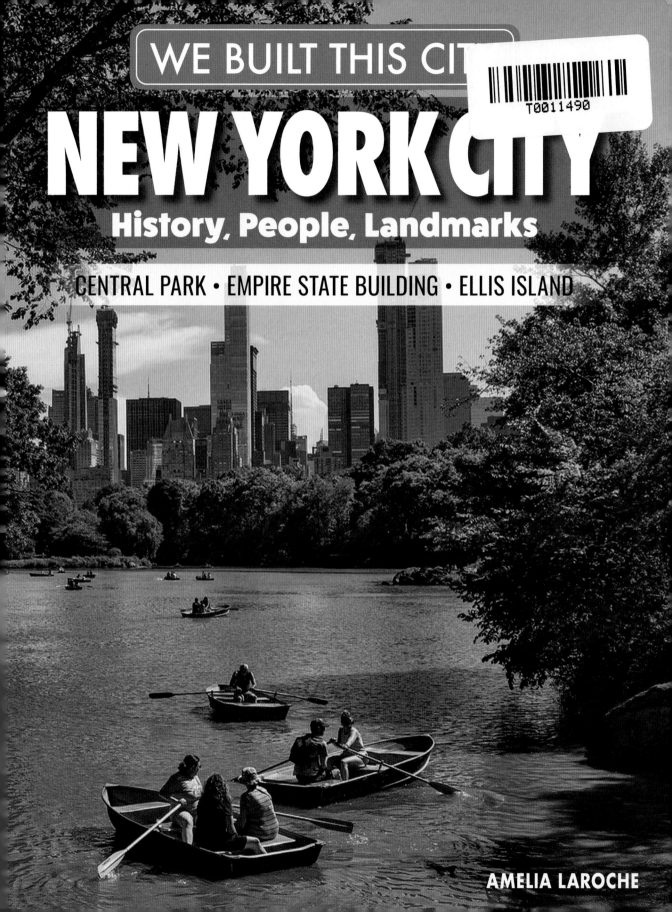

WE BUILT THIS CITY

NEW YORK CITY
History, People, Landmarks

CENTRAL PARK • EMPIRE STATE BUILDING • ELLIS ISLAND

AMELIA LAROCHE

Paperback ISBN 979-8-89094-050-6
Hardcover ISBN 979-8-89094-051-3

Library of Congress Control Number: 2023943821

To learn more about the other great books from Fox Chapel Publishing, or to find a retailer near you, call toll-free 800-457-9112 or visit us at *www.FoxChapelPublishing.com*.

We are always looking for talented authors. To submit an idea, please send a brief inquiry to acquisitions@foxchapelpublishing.com.

Fox Chapel Publishing makes every effort to use environmentally friendly paper for printing.

Printed in China

ABOUT THE AUTHOR: Amelia LaRoche lived in the Hell's Kitchen neighborhood of Manhattan for over a decade. She now lives in Maine, where she works for a newspaper. She has written several children's books on topics ranging from the country of France to the wild world of parrots.

NEW YORK CITY

 New York City, New York

 1st largest city in the USA

 302.6 square miles

 Population: 8.47 million

 Elevation: 33 ft.

 Settled: 1624

New York City
is known as
"The Big Apple"

New York City stands as a sprawling testament to ambition, diversity, and the relentless pursuit of dreams. Its iconic skyline, with the towering Empire State Building, inspiring Statue of Liberty, and the brilliant lights of Times Square, draw millions of visitors from around the world. The city's historic roots run deep and rich. From the Dutch settlers who founded New Amsterdam to the immigrants who passed through Ellis Island seeking a better life, NYC is a tapestry of diverse neighborhoods. Explore this global center for commerce, culture, and creativity from the theaters of Broadway, the fresh air of Central Park, and the many museums, to the unique enclaves of Chinatown, Little Italy, and Harlem. Welcome to New York!

CONTENTS

Chapter One
The City That Never Sleeps
7

Chapter Two
Fur Wars
11

Chapter Three
A New Home Called New York
17

Chapter Four
Building Boom
23

Chapter Five
I Love New York
31

Chronology • 37
Further Reading • 38
Glossary • 39
Index • 40

Science and engineering marvels abound in New York City, from the bones of a triceratops in the American Museum of Natural History to the Statue of Liberty and the elevators that take visitors to the top of the Empire State Building.

Chapter One

The City That Never Sleeps

Imagine you've just had the busiest and most exciting week of your life on your first trip to New York City. You stood on the dizzying 102nd floor of the Empire State Building, so high above Manhattan that the yellow taxicabs below looked like ants. You used chopsticks to eat dumplings in Chinatown. You took a ferry to the Statue of Liberty in New York Harbor. And you took a train to Coney Island in Brooklyn, where you rode the most famous wooden roller coaster in the world: the 60-mile-per-hour Cyclone.[1] Then you saw ancient mummies and towering, toothy dinosaur skeletons at the American Museum of Natural History.

And today, on your last full day, you visited Central Park, where you sat atop a gleaming white horse on the carousel, laughed at the waddling penguins in Central Park Zoo, and cheered for your favorite model sailboat in a race at Conservatory Water.

Now, just outside the park, you stop at a street vendor's cart to buy a huge, salty pretzel. As you bite into the warm, soft dough, you check your subway map to figure out which train you'll take back to your hotel in SoHo. The helpful hotel concierge taught you that SoHo got its name because the neighborhood is SOuth of HOuston Street. "You say it 'how,' as in 'How-ston' Street," she had whispered, back on your first day, when you pronounced it "HYOO-ston," like the city in Texas.

As you wash down your pretzel with a gulp of cold root beer, you notice that the sidewalks on Fifth Avenue are blocked off. Suddenly, a dozen police motorcycles roar down the wide street. Long black

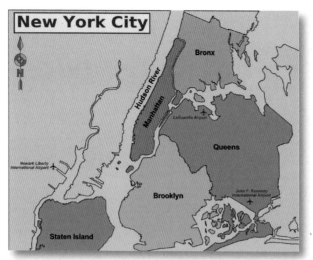

New York City lies on the East Coast of the United States, where the Hudson River meets the Atlantic Ocean.

limousines follow them. It's the Prime Minister of England, in town to give a speech at the United Nations!

From parks to pretzels to visiting leaders, after all you've seen and done, now you know why they call New York the City That Never Sleeps.

New York City is home to over 8 million people[2] packed into five boroughs:

Manhattan, Brooklyn, the Bronx, Queens, and Staten Island. It has the most people of any city in the U.S., more than twice as many as the second most populated city, Los Angeles. Around 1 in every 38 people in the United States is a New Yorker. But the Big Apple wasn't always so built-up and busy.

Five hundred years ago, it was green and hilly, with marshes, meadows, and woods. The land was home to the Lenape, which means "the People." For hundreds of generations, the Lenape had everything they needed to live in harmony with the land. They moved

The Lenape called the Hudson River "Shatemuc," or "the river that flows both ways," because its flow changes with the ocean's tides.

Lenape dwellings like this could be found on the lands that would become New York.

from place to place, spending time in campsites near the shore to fish and gather clams and oysters in summer. They moved inland to harvest their crops of maize, beans, melons, and tobacco, and to hunt deer and other animals in fall. When winter set in, they moved to more protected places, and spent time together in longhouses. They took only what they needed from the land, and after they left a campsite, the land could rest and animal populations could rebound.

The Lenape were grouped according to their mothers' clans, which were named after animals common to the area: turtle, turkey, or wolf. Mountain lions, deer, mink, and black bears also roamed this region. More than 150 species of birds chattered in forests filled with at least 70 kinds of trees. Dolphins and whales swam in what would come to be called Hudson Bay. Herring, trout, and eels filled the rivers. There were so many beavers that Dutch fur traders would eventually be able to build a business around them, and beavers would be pictured on the seal of New York City.

Many places in the region still have Lenape or Lenape-inspired names, such as the Canarsie neighborhood in Brooklyn and Raritan Bay. The paths the Lenape moved on became paved roads still used today, including Broadway in Manhattan. If you walk there, you can be pretty sure that hundreds of years ago, a Lenape your age walked on the same spot.

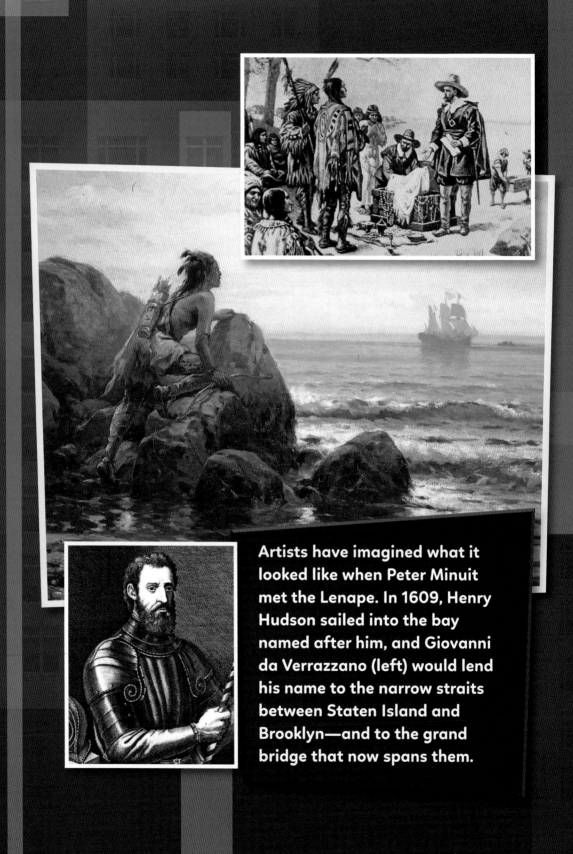

Artists have imagined what it looked like when Peter Minuit met the Lenape. In 1609, Henry Hudson sailed into the bay named after him, and Giovanni da Verrazzano (left) would lend his name to the narrow straits between Staten Island and Brooklyn—and to the grand bridge that now spans them.

Fur Wars

In 1524, Italian explorer Giovanni da Verrazzano sailed across the Atlantic Ocean, looking for a shortcut to China. He anchored in the Narrows between Staten Island and Brooklyn. The bridge joining Staten Island and Brooklyn is named after him: the Verrazzano-Narrows Bridge. When it was originally opened in 1964, the Triborough Bridge and Tunnel Authority got the name wrong, spelling it as the *Verrazano*-Narrows Bridge.

On a sunny September day in 1609, Henry Hudson and his crew of Dutch and English sailors on the Halve Maen (Half Moon) spotted Mannahatta ("island hill"). They, too, were looking for a shortcut to Asia. They didn't find a route to China's silks and spices, but they did find riches of another kind: beaver pelts.

In Europe, people loved wearing beaver fur. They used it to line their coats and to make collars, hats, and sleigh blankets. It was warm, durable, and pretty. In 1624, the Dutch West India Company sent 30 families to settle on "Nutten Island" (today's Governors Island, between Lower Manhattan and Brooklyn).

Two years later, their governor, Peter Minuit, offered the Lenape a handful of goods, including farming equipment and cloth, in exchange for Manhattan. The Lenape didn't believe land could be owned—they believed it was there for everyone to use—but they accepted Minuit's goods. The Dutch called their home New Amsterdam.

New Amsterdam. Wall Street, the center of finance, got its name from an actual wall the Dutch built there for protection.

The beaver trade made some people rich, and it also ruined lives. From 1626 to 1632, ships carried more than 52,500 pelts to the Netherlands.[1] The beaver trade changed the way the Lenape and other tribes of the region lived. Men who used to hunt for their families started traveling farther and staying away longer. The beaver population plummeted.

In 1664, the English grabbed New Amsterdam from the Dutch and named it New York, in honor of their Duke of York back home. For the next hundred years, the population grew and became more diverse. It included immigrants from Western Europe and people taken from Africa as slaves. Indentured servants came mainly from England. They

The Wyckoff House in Canarsie, Brooklyn, is New York's oldest standing house. It was built by Pieter Claeson Wyckoff, who sailed over from Germany almost 400 years ago.

promised to work for several years without payment in exchange for a boat ride to the New World.

From 1754 to 1763, the French and Indian War raged between British American colonists and French Canadian colonists, with different native tribes choosing sides. A 22-year-old soldier named George Washington got battleground experience that he would use in the next war: the American Revolution.

That revolution was a direct result of the French and Indian War. The British levied taxes in the colonies to help pay for the war. The colonists refused to pay. They said the taxes weren't fair, because they had no members in the British Parliament. Why should they pay taxes if they couldn't also help make the laws—including the laws about who should pay taxes? In 1776, with this conflict in full swing, the Continental Congress adopted the Declaration of Independence. It said the colonies would no longer be ruled by Britain. Instead, they would be an independent country.

For the next several years, British forces and the Continental Army fought. The British occupied New York City until 1783, when both sides signed a treaty that ended the war. On November 25, Evacuation Day, the last British troops sailed out of New York. A British warship fired the final shot of the American Revolution at Staten Island's Fort Wadsworth, where jeering crowds had gathered to watch the intruders leave. The shot fell short and landed in the water.

Fort Wadsworth, on Staten Island, was the target of the final shot of the American Revolution.

George Washington gets sworn in as president.

In 1785, New York City became the capital of what was now the United States. Four years later, hundreds of excited citizens gathered outside Federal Hall on Wall Street in Manhattan. The date was April 30, 1789, and starting at 9 a.m., church bells around the city rang for half an hour. At 2 p.m., an older and wiser George Washington, wearing a brown suit with buttons showing eagles with wings spread, placed one hand on a Bible and took an oath to become the first president of the United States.

A fire on December 16, 1835, destroyed 17 blocks including many buildings in the South Street Seaport on the East River. They were soon rebuilt and by 1850, the port was busier than ever. At the time, New York had the nation's busiest maritime trade.

A New Home Called New York

By 1800, New York had become a booming center of trading, banking, and shipping. The 363-mile Erie Canal from Lake Erie to the Hudson River was completed in 1825, making New York the trading capital of the nation.

New York Harbor played a big role in the cotton market: Southern planters sent their crops to East River docks, where they were shipped to mills in England. The mills shipped back finished cloth. Garment workers in Manhattan sewed some of it into clothing for slaves in the South.

In 1861, the Civil War pitted North against South, and in New York, people were divided about which side to take. When Congress passed a law saying that all white men between the ages of 20 and 45 could be drafted and forced to fight, tensions mounted. The Draft Riots of 1863 were the most violent riots in the city's history. What started as a protest against the draft turned into a race riot. For five days, thousands of angry white men, women, and even children attacked black neighborhoods. The riots were finally quelled, but not before at least 105 people were killed.[1]

After the Civil War, slavery was outlawed. Many African Americans moved from the South to find jobs in the North. Immigration from Europe also increased, and New York became the first stop for millions of people seeking a new life in the United States. Travelers

Ellis Island was sometimes called "The Island of Tears" because not every immigrant who made the long voyage was admitted to the United States.

from Ireland, Germany, Poland, Italy, Russia, and other countries packed their belongings and climbed onto steamships, knowing they might never see their home countries again.

The Statue of Liberty raised her torch above New York Harbor to welcome the immigrants. Between 1892 and 1954, more than 12 million people passed through the inspection station on tiny Ellis Island, a stone's throw from the statue's home on Liberty Island.[2]

Many of these people worked in New York's factories and mills for twelve or more hours a day, six days a week. The factories were called "sweatshops," because sweat is what people did in these hot and often dangerous workplaces. It took a deadly fire at a factory owned by the Triangle Shirtwaist Company in March 1911 to bring about change. The workers on the top three floors of the Asch Building in Manhattan were immigrant women—many of them teenagers—who worked all day in front of whirring sewing machines.

When the fire broke out, the workers were trapped. There was only one working elevator, and it could hold only 12 people. Of the two exit doors, one was locked and the other opened inward. Panicked women were crushed as they piled against it trying to escape. The building's single fire escape collapsed. All told, 146 workers died. The nation demanded that labor laws be changed.

Four decades earlier, housing laws had also been reformed. Underpaid workers had often been packed into crowded, dark tenements, usually located near the factories where they worked. In 1867, New York State passed a law that improved living conditions. Called the Tenement House Act, it even required that every room have a window. That law still exists in New York City's building codes.

While the city was making room for the newcomers, planners also found ways to preserve hundreds of acres of parkland. In 1858, Frederick

Olmsted designed Central Park for pedestrians, carriages, relaxation, and entertainment. Bridges and buildings were built of local stone, and plantings were to look natural, not like a garden. Four roads cross Central Park, but they are hidden by foliage.

Mulberry Street, running right through the Manhattan neighborhood of Little Italy and then on to Chinatown, was on New York City maps as early as 1755. By 1900, it was bustling with a diverse population of immigrants.

Law Olmsted and Calvert Vaux designed Central Park in Manhattan. Eight years later, they created Prospect Park in Brooklyn.

The city was constantly changing, with groups spreading north, building new neighborhoods, and then moving on. The neighborhood of Harlem began as a farming town. When the railroad connected this northern part of the island to the busy southern tip, and the elevated train lines came in the late 1870s, neighborhoods built up fast. Jewish immigrants from Eastern Europe and Italian immigrants moved to Harlem by the thousands.

African Americans also swelled the population of Harlem, especially after 1904, when homes lost their value and landlords had trouble filling them. Phillip Payton Jr., who owned the Afro-American Realty Company, saw an opportunity. He convinced black people to move to Harlem not

The Harlem Renaissance of the 1920s was a blossoming of artistic, intellectual, and social expression.

only from other parts of the city, but also from the South, to take advantage of the empty homes. During the 1920s and 1930s, black culture thrived in Harlem. In 1921, a bookstore devoted to black literature, Young's Book Exchange, opened, and many more followed. Theaters, dance halls, and supper clubs featured dancers and musicians who played swing and jazz. They attracted audiences from all over the city and beyond.

With all these new arrivals to the city, New York was getting crowded. Developers didn't have room to build "out," so instead, they built "up."

Just before the start of the 20th century, residents of Queens, the Bronx, Staten Island, and Brooklyn—all independent cities at that time—voted to join with Manhattan to form Greater New York. When people went to bed on December 31, 1897, New York City had 2 million people; when they woke up the next day, on January 1, 1898, the plan was in effect. The city boasted 3.3 million residents, and at 360 square miles, it had grown six times larger.[3]

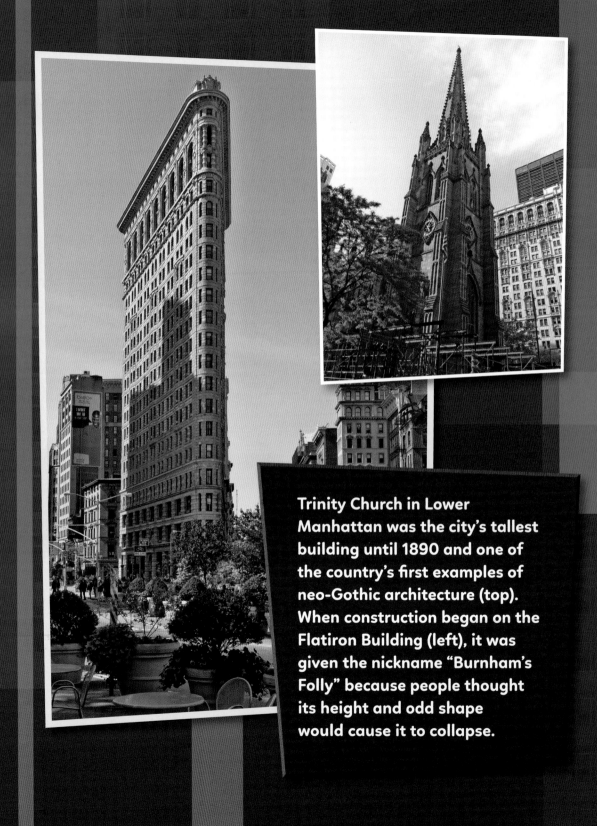

Trinity Church in Lower Manhattan was the city's tallest building until 1890 and one of the country's first examples of neo-Gothic architecture (top). When construction began on the Flatiron Building (left), it was given the nickname "Burnham's Folly" because people thought its height and odd shape would cause it to collapse.

Building Boom

In 1888, architect Bradford Lee Gilbert had a problem. He was hired to design an 11-story office building on Broadway, but the lot was only 21.5 feet wide. If he used the traditional bearing-wall construction of the day, the walls would have to be so thick that there would be only eight feet of free space across the ground floor. Gilbert had worked on the railroad, designing stations and terminals. He had a bright idea: Why not turn a railroad bridge on end, and support the floors and outside walls on strong iron girders? The Tower Building opened in 1889. Gilbert wasn't the first to build skyward, but his way of making the most of the space he was given became a New York City hallmark.

New inventions—the elevator and electricity—were letting architects in Chicago and New York build what would come to be called "skyscrapers." The 130-foot-tall Equitable Life Assurance Building on Broadway was the world's first to have a passenger elevator when it was completed in 1870.

"Tallest" was still a boast that could be made by Trinity Church in Lower Manhattan. Its Gothic spire rose to 281 feet.

Not the tallest, but among New York's best-known skyscrapers even today, was the Flatiron Building completed in 1902. It rose 22 stories to 285 feet. Like Gilbert with the Tower Building, architects Daniel Burnham and Frederick P. Dinkelberg made the most of what they were given: a wedge-shaped plot of land at the intersection of Fifth Avenue and Broadway. One reason for its nickname was because

The Chrysler Building

the Flatiron was shaped like an iron. It was only six feet wide at the tip.

Three years after a disastrous fire burned the Equitable Building in 1912, a new one was built in its place. It had the most office space of any building in the world, enough for 16,000 workers. The 1.25 million-square-foot, 40-story building was packed onto less than an acre. People nearby complained that it was throwing their homes into constant shadow. Worries that New York was getting too built-up too fast led to the Zoning Resolution of 1916, the United States' first citywide building code.

The codes required setbacks above a certain height. The art deco Chrysler Building in 1930 and Empire State Building in 1931 used these setbacks, making them look like tiered wedding cakes.

The most important materials in New York City's buildings—besides steel and concrete—were money and ambition. Men made rich from the growing railroad, oil, and other industries would shape not just the skyline, but also the cultural life of the city we know today.

Andrew Carnegie (pronounced kar-NAY-ghee) grew up poor in Scotland. His family moved to Pennsylvania in 1848 when he was twelve. His hardworking mother repaired shoes to keep the family fed, and he vowed to give her an easier life. Carnegie made a fortune in the iron and steel business, when the booming railroad and construction industries

A construction worker high above Manhattan bolts together beams on the Empire State Building.

needed raw materials. In 1901, he sold Carnegie Steel Company to banker John Pierpont Morgan for $480 million. Then he figured out how to give away more than $350 million (the equivalent of billions in today's dollars).

An avid reader, he infused the New York Public Library system with cash. He gave $1.1 million to build Carnegie Hall. This now-legendary concert venue opened in 1891.

Another tycoon, John D. Rockefeller, also rose from rags to riches. He founded the Standard Oil Company. Like Carnegie,

Carnegie Hall houses three concert halls and a museum. When a larger hall was added in the year 2000, workers had to dig down into the ground, removing enough dirt to fill 363 garbage trucks.

The ice-skating rink at Rockefeller Center attracts skaters of every age.

he also gave away a lot of his money, but much of his wealth went to his only son, John Jr.

John D. Rockefeller Jr. donated property on West 54th Street for the site of the Museum of Modern Art, which his wife, Abigail, had founded in 1929. He also built low-rent housing in poor sections of the city.

During the Great Depression in the 1930s, he built Rockefeller Center. The 14-building plan created 75,000 jobs at a time when work was hard to find. Rockefeller Center now contains Radio City Music Hall, where the Rockettes kick up their heels every year during their Christmas show.

After World War II, Rockefeller donated land for the

Radio City Music Hall was designated as a New York City Landmark in 1978 and renovated in 1999.

United Nations headquarters. In 1958 he provided $5 million to build the Lincoln Center for the Performing Arts.

Since the 1950s, the city has continued to change. City planners, including Robert Moses, added beauty and function with more bridges, parks, and parkways. Interstate highways made it easier to work in the city but live in the suburbs. Many people moved out of New York, and the city struggled. Then, the Hart-Celler Immigration and Nationality Act of 1965 made it possible for immigrants from Asia, Africa, the Caribbean, and Latin America to come to the United

Leaders from all over the world often meet at the United Nations Secretariat Building in Manhattan.

The Lincoln Center's Metropolitan Opera House glows against the New York City skyline.

States. Many of these newcomers settled in New York City, bringing neighborhoods back to life.

Factories also left the city, but jobs in the service industries grew. Today, Wall Street provides jobs for brokers, bankers, and other office workers. The city boasts more than 100 colleges, including New York University, Columbia University, and the City University of New York. Thousands of medical professionals work in the city's world-class hospitals, including NewYork-Presbyterian and Mount Sinai. The tourist industry is booming.

In the late 1990s, the city found ways to use the abandoned factory buildings in neighborhoods like the Meatpacking District and Chelsea in

Columbia University is known to be a world-class research institution.

Manhattan. Many were converted into large studios for artists, and into shops and restaurants. A converted area in Brooklyn is nicknamed DUMBO. It stands for "Down Under the Manhattan Bridge Overpass." Stretching along the East River, it has huge apartments and stunning views of downtown Manhattan.

DUMBO also has fine art galleries, high quality eateries, and outdoor spaces like Brooklyn Bridge Park.

Today, the city is a more popular place to live than ever. The monthly average rent for a two-bedroom apartment in Manhattan is just over $4,500. And for some people, there is no limit to what they will spend to own prime real estate. In 2015, a duplex penthouse at One57, a condominium on West 57th Street, sold for over $100 million.[1]

The New York Stock Exchange on Wall Street sets the pace for the nation's economy.

One World Trade Center
and the pools at the
National September 11
Memorial & Museum were
completed in 2014.

I Love New York

At the southern tip of Manhattan, One World Trade Center soars 104 stories into the sky. The tower stands at 1,776 feet (a height chosen because that's the year the Declaration of Independence was signed). It is the tallest building in the entire western hemisphere and the seventh tallest in the world.

It contains 73 elevators, including the ones that carry passengers to the observatory. Those shoot up 1,250 feet in 47 seconds, while screens on the elevator walls show time-lapse images of Manhattan over the last 500 years, from its days as marshland to now.[1]

One World Trade Center is part of the World Trade Center complex, which contains other glassy skyscrapers that are already built or being planned. Half of it is dedicated to the National September 11 Memorial & Museum. It commemorates the September 11, 2001 attacks by terrorists, who flew two planes into the Twin Towers that once stood there. The memorial consists of two large pools placed in the footprints of the Twin Towers. Water cascades down all four sides of each pool, and the names of the victims are carved in bronze on the low walls surrounding them.

Below ground at the World Trade Center is the Transportation Hub, with access to 12 subway lines, PATH trains to New Jersey, and retailers, and within walking distance to the ferries chugging out of Battery Park. Sometimes called the Oculus, it opened in March 2016. It serves some 250,000 PATH commuters on an average weekday. Even more people, 750,000 a day, scurry through Grand Central Terminal in midtown Manhattan. Commuters swell Manhattan's population from 1.6 million to 3.1 million every weekday.[2]

People don't just commute to New York. In 2016, more than 60 million people visited the Big Apple.[3]

Tourists come for many reasons. There are amazing sights, like neon-lit Times Square. This area burns 161 megawatts of electricity at once, twice as much as all of the casinos in Las Vegas put together.[4] There are classic Broadway shows, such as *Chicago* and *The Phantom of the Opera*, which finished a historic 35-year run in 2023. For newer shows, like *Hamilton*, the best seats can cost up to $850.

Times Square is also known as "the Great White Way" because Broadway was one of the first streets to be lit by electricity.

New York is famous for its parades, including the Lunar New Year Parade that winds through Chinatown every year.

There are parades: dragons wind through Chinatown during Chinese New Year, the St. Patrick's Day Parade breaks out the bagpipes in March, the Mermaid Parade swims along the streets of Coney Island in June, ghouls and goblins haunt the Village Halloween Parade, and giant floats bob above Sixth Avenue during the Macy's Thanksgiving Day Parade.

For the sporty, the Mets play baseball at Citi Field in Queens, and the Yankees play in the Bronx. In Madison Square Garden, the Knicks shoot hoops and the Rangers strap on hockey skates. For the dapper, there is Fashion Week, long held in Bryant Park, and now hosted at the Lincoln Center for the Performing Arts, where million-dollar models strut the runway in glamorous gowns.

Madison Square Garden hosts basketball and ice hockey games, as well as huge concerts and comedy shows.

The city continues to become more eco-friendly and livable. In 2009, the Empire State Building made energy-saving improvements. Since then, it has saved nearly 40 percent of its energy and $4.4 million every year.

Cars and trucks are now banned from parts of Broadway, and in their place, pedestrian plazas with street furniture have been added at Times Square and Herald Square. Bicycle lanes have also been improved.

A great way to explore New York City is to rent a bicycle through the Citi Bike bike share program!

More than one-third of New Yorkers were born outside the United States.

There is one thing you can read about, but that you can't truly understand until you feel it for yourself: It is the energy of New York City, of being around so many different people, from all walks of life, from everywhere in the world. There are celebrities and young dreamers: actors, dancers, filmmakers, and writers. There are fat-cat Wall Street bankers, oil tycoons, and dot-com billionaires. There are the people who make up the backbone of the city: firefighters, nurses, janitors, construction workers, taxi drivers, teachers, and other everyday heroes.

The writer E. B. White said of New York City, "It can destroy an individual, or it can fulfill him, depending a good deal on luck. No one should come to New York to live unless he is willing to be lucky."[5] So if your dream is to come to New York, ask yourself: Am I ready to be lucky?

Chronology

1600s Europeans meet the Lenape, or Lenni-Lenape, who have been living along the east coast of North America for thousands of years.

1754 The French and Indian War is fought between England and France for control of territory in North America. The British win, with France losing control of Canada. The British impose taxes on the American Colonies to pay for the war; this leads to the American Revolution.

1792 Twenty-four stockbrokers meet under a shady buttonwood tree on Wall Street in lower Manhattan and sign an agreement that will lead to the formation of the New York Stock & Exchange Board in 1817. Today it is known simply as the New York Stock Exchange, and it is the largest in the world. Trading of everything from coffee to computers still begins every weekday with the ringing of a loud bell.

1825 The Erie Canal is finished. It connects Lake Erie to the Hudson River.

1883 After 13 years of construction, the Brooklyn Bridge opens. The following year, showman P.T. Barnum leads a parade of 21 elephants and 17 camels across the bridge to prove it is sturdy.

1885 The U.S. Army Corps of Engineers sets off 300,000 pounds of explosives to blow up Flood Rock and make it easier to ship things through Hell Gate, a narrow part of the East River. People in distant Princeton, New Jersey, feel the blast.

1898 The five boroughs join to become Greater New York.

1899 The Bronx Zoo opens. Today it includes a Treetop Adventure that lets kids 7 and older zipline over the Bronx River.

1904 New York City's first subway line, called the IRT, opens.

1911 The tragedy of the Triangle Shirtwaist Factory fire prompts the city to create laws that will make working conditions safer.

1916 New York passes the Zoning Resolution of 1916, the first citywide code in the United States.

1952 New York City becomes the permanent headquarters of the United Nations.

1969 The Stonewall riots break out in Manhattan, sparking the beginning of the fight for gay rights in the United States.

1973 The World Trade Center is completed. The taller of the Twin Towers stands 1,368 feet high.

1977 The I LOVE NEW YORK tourism campaign is born. A blackout pitches most of the city into darkness for 25 hours. Criminals set hundreds of fires and steal from thousands of stores.

1989 David Dinkins is elected as the first African-American mayor of New York City.

2001 On September 11, terrorists fly into the Twin Towers at the World Trade Center, demolishing the buildings and killing nearly 3,000 people.

Chronology

2012   In October, Hurricane Sandy causes widespread destruction. Jane's Carousel in Brooklyn Bridge Park survives the storm and becomes a symbol of the strength of the city.

2018   The minimum wage in New York City climbs to $15 by the end of the year (for companies with more than 11 workers). Laws are passed that make it easier for new parents to take time off from work, with pay.

2020   The murder of George Floyd prompts protests in the city and throughout the world. Sandra Lindsay, an RN at Long Island Jewish Medical Center, receives the first COVID-19 vaccine dose.

CHAPTER 1. THE CITY THAT NEVER SLEEPS

1. Donnelly, Tim. "Is This the Most Dangerous Roller Coaster in America?" *New York Post*, July 18, 2015. https://nypost.com/2015/07/18/is-this-the-most-dangerous-roller-coaster-in-america/
2. United States Census Bureau. "Quick Facts: New York City, New York." https://www.census.gov/quickfacts/fact/table/newyorkcitynewyork/PST045222

CHAPTER 2. FUR WARS

1. New Netherland Institute: "A Tour of New Netherland: Fur Trade." https://www.newnetherlandinstitute.org/history-and-heritage/digital-exhibitions/a-tour-of-new-netherland/hudson-river/fur-trade/

CHAPTER 3. A NEW HOME CALLED NEW YORK

1. Wheeler, Linda. "The New York Draft Riots of 1863." *The Washington Post*, April 29, 2013. https://www.washingtonpost.com/lifestyle/style/the-new-york-draft-riots-of-1863/2013/04/26/a1aacf52-a620-11e2-a8e2-5b98cb59187f_story.html
2. "Three Spectacular Museums in New York City." *Impressive Magazine*, July 31, 2013.
3. Maeder, Jay. Big Town, Big Time: A New York Epic: 1898–1998. (New York: *The New York Daily News*, 1999), p. 7.

CHAPTER 4. BUILDING BOOM

1. Willett, Megan. "Inside One57, Where New York's Most Expensive Penthouse Just Sold for a Record-Breaking $100 Million." *Business Insider*, January 20, 2015. https://www.businessinsider.com/inside-one57s-100-million-penthouse-2015-1

CHAPTER 5. I LOVE NEW YORK

1. Yuhas, Alan. "One World Trade Center Elevators Offer 500-Year History Ride—In 47 Seconds." *The Guardian*, April 20, 2015. https://www.theguardian.com/us-news/2015/apr/20/one-world-trade-center-elevators-500-
2. Metcalfe, John. "The Many Ways People Commute to New York." *Bloomberg CityLab*, September 26, 2016. https://www.bloomberg.com/news/articles/2016-09-26/mapping-how-people-commute-to-manhattan
3. Plitt, Amy. "NYC Tourism to Hit Record Numbers in 2017." Curbed, NY, November 20, 2017. https://ny.curbed.com/2017/11/20/16678672/new-york-tourism-2017-nyc-and-company
4. Bouey, Steve. "The Power to Light Up Times Square." *The World By Road*, July 2013. https://theworldbyroad.com/2013/7/the-power-to-light-up-times-square/
5. White, E. B. *Here Is New York* (New York: Harper & Brothers Publishers, 1949.)

Further Reading

Works Consulted

Burrows, Edwin G., & Mike Wallace. Gotham: *A History of New York City to 1898*. New York: Oxford University Press, 1999.

Danigelis, Alyssa. "NYC's Empire State Building Takes Energy-Efficiency to New Heights." *Energy Manager Today*, September 25, 2017.

Filler, Martin. "New York: Conspicuous Construction." *The New York Review*. April 2, 2015. https://www.nybooks.com/articles/2015/04/02/new-york-conspicuous-construction/

Harris, Leslie M. "The New York City Draft Riots of 1863," excerpted from pages 279–288 of *In the Shadow of Slavery: African Americans in New York City*, 1626–1863. Chicago: University of Chicago Press, 2004.

Mount Vernon Ladies' Association. "President Washington's Inauguration." © 2018. https://www.mountvernon.org/george-washington/the-first-president/inauguration/timeline

Nelson, Rob. "Times Square Celebrates Spring Opening of New Pedestrian Plazas." Eyewitness News, April 19, 2017. https://abc7ny.com/news/times-square-celebrates-spring-opening-of-new-pedestrian-plazas/1892392/

New York Historical Society. "New York Divided: Slavery and the Civil War." www.nydivided.org

Quinn, Helen. "How Ancient Collision Shaped New York Skyline." *BBC News: Science & Environment*, June 7, 2013. https://www.bbc.com/news/science-environment-22798563

Sanburn, Josh. "The Top of America." *Time*, March 6, 2014. https://time.com/13828/the-top-of-america/

Sanderson, Eric W. *Mannahatta: A Natural History of New York City*. New York: Abrams, 2009.

World Trade Center. https://www.wtc.com

Wyckoff House Museum, Brooklyn. http://wyckoffmuseum.org/about/history/

On the Internet

Central Park History
https://www.american-historama.org/1850-1860-secession-era/central-park.htm

Ellis Island History Facts
https://www.american-historama.org/1881-1913-maturation-era/ellis-island-history-facts.htm

The Nanticoke Lenni-Lenape
https://nanticoke-lenape.info/history.htm

Glossary

architect (AR-kih-tekt)—A person who designs buildings.

century (SEN-chur-ee)—A period of 100 years. You can remember how long a century is by remembering that there are 100 cents in a dollar.

concierge (KON-see-ayrj)—An employee who helps hotel guests find fun things to do.

condominium (kon-doh-MIH-nee-um)—A building (or group of buildings) containing units owned by individuals.

congress (KON-gress)—A group of people who make the laws that everyone has to follow. The members are elected by the citizens.

diverse (dy-VERS)—Showing a variety.

eco-friendly (EE-koh frend-lee)—Not harmful to the environment.

foundation (fown-DAY-shun)—The bottom part of a building that holds all the weight; most foundations are below ground.

girder (GIR-der)—A beam made of iron or steel used to build bridges or the framework of large buildings.

hemisphere (HEH-mis-feer)—Half of a sphere. Earth is a sphere. People divide earth into the Eastern and Western Hemispheres. The Western Hemisphere contains North, Central, and South America.

immigrant (IH-mih-grint)—A person who comes to live permanently in a foreign country.

indentured (in-DEN-churd)—Forced to work for someone for a specific period of time in order to repay a debt.

longhouse (LONG-hous)—A long, narrow, single-room building used by groups of families around the world. Lenape longhouses had a frame made from bent saplings covered in bark.

reinforced (ree-in-FORST)—Having extra strength added, such as steel bars set in concrete to make it stronger.

revolution (reh-vuh-LOO-shun)—The overthrow of one system in favor of another.

shirtwaist (SHIRT-wayst)—A woman's blouse or dress with buttons down the front or back.

venue (VEN-yoo)—The place where events or activities are held.

Index

African Americans 17, 20, 36

American Museum of Natural History 6–7

beavers 9, 11–12

Broadway 3, 9, 23, 32, 34

Bronx 8, 21, 33, 36

Brooklyn 7–11, 13, 20–21, 29, 36–37

Bryant Park 33

Burnham, Daniel 22–23

Carnegie, Andrew 24–25

Carnegie Hall 25

Central Park 3, 7, 19–20

Chinatown 3, 7, 20, 33

Chrysler Building 24

City University of New York 28

Columbia University 28

Coney Island 7, 33

Cyclone 7

Draft Riots of 1863 17, 36

Dutch West India Company 11

Ellis Island 3, 18

Empire State Building 3, 6–7, 24–25, 34

Equitable Life Assurance Building 23–24

Fifth Avenue 7, 23

Flatiron Building 22–24

Gilbert, Bradford Lee 23

Governors Island 11

Grand Central Terminal 31

Harlem 3, 20–21

Hart-Cellar Immigration and Nationality Act of 1965 27

Hudson, Henry 10–11

Hudson River 8, 17, 36

Lenape 8–12, 36, 39

Liberty Island 18

Lincoln Center for the Performing Arts 27, 33

Madison Square Garden 33–34

Manhattan 7–9, 11, 15, 17–18, 20–23, 25, 27, 29, 31–32, 36–37

Minuit, Peter 10–11

Morgan, John Pierpont 25

Moses, Robert 27

Museum of Modern Art 26

National September 11 Memorial & Museum 30–31

New Amsterdam 3, 11–12

New York Harbor 7, 17–18

New York Public Library 25

New York University 28

Olmstead, Frederick Law 19–20

PATH trains 31

Payton, Phillip, Jr. 20

Prospect Park 20

Queens 8, 21, 33

Radio City Music Hall 26

Rockefeller, John D. 25

Rockefeller, John D., Jr. 26

Rockefeller Center 26

SoHo 7

South Street Seaport 16

Staten Island 8, 10–11, 14, 21

Statue of Liberty 3, 6–7, 18

Tenement House Act 19

Times Square 3, 32, 34

Tower Building 23

Triangle Shirtwaist Company 18, 36

Triborough Bridge and Tunnel Authority 11

Trinity Church 22–23

United Nations 8, 27, 36

Vaux, Calvert 20

Verrazzano, Giovanni da 10–11

Verrazzano-Narrows Bridge 11

Wall Street 12, 15, 28–29, 35–36

Washington, George 13, 15

White, E.B. 35

World Trade Center 30–31, 36

Wyckoff, Pieter Claeson 13

Young's Book Exchange 21

Zoning Resolution of 1916 24, 36